MW00941863

MALICE

with a Purpose...

How to PROTECT yourself from PHYSICAL
AGGRESSION EMOTIONAL DISTRESS
UNTHETICAL PROFESSIONALS
without, being NAÏVE, but SMART

Onofre Jusino, Ph.D.

Malice with a Purpose
How to protect yourself from physical aggression,
emotional distress and unethical professionals without
being naïve, but smart

Copyright © 2018 by Onofre Jusino

Printed in the United States of America
ISBN-13: 978-1985054707

DEDICATION

To My Wonderful Family
and to the GOOD people that have been
mistreated, bullied and abused
by those toxic ones, because
of their lack of malice...

CONTENTS

PROLOGUE

The principal purpose of this book is to teach the good but sometimes NAIVE people, how to defend themselves PHYSICALLY and LEGALLY from those with bad intentions or evil mentality. These toxic people include, bullies, murderers, rapists, all kinds of criminals, and "unethical-professionals," bosses, competitors, lawyers, co-workers, contractors, neighbors, etc.

MALICE with a PURPOSE will show you the procedure of total self-defense, integrated into a global system of prevention and actions that will prepare you against those acting with malice against you. Sometimes being too polite, "sweet" and friendly is confused for weakness and some people take advantage of that. It is a matter of choosing the correct people to be around you and avoiding the TOXIC

> *Avoiding SMALL problems will take you out of the BIG ones.*

ones, even if they are members of your family and here you will learn how.

Malice with a Purpose will teach you how to gain respect from others as well as to develop an INTUITION of being alert, smart and with the legal malice to defend yourself and your loved ones and to stop being NAIVE and abused by those that have malice ON purpose.

> "If a man means to kill you, strike first"
> The Talmud

In this book you will learn how to recognize bad people and bad situations and in case of a physical confrontation, you will learn how to neutralize an attacker in less than ONE second and with just ONE movement. Your age, sex and/or physical condition is irrelevant because it is done using just three "factors" that if kept in mind, they will become your "stealth" weapon of self-defense.

General Information

For a physical defense always remember these three factors.

- WHEN to attack
- HOW to attack

- WHERE to attack

When these three factors and others, that I will teach you, concerning how to defend yourself will be explained, you will be equipped with the knowledge that will help you to ALWAYS defend yourself with self-confidence, step-by-step.

Make this method a part of your daily thinking and it will become yours as a mental arsenal of self-defense so when the time comes, showing you the word of "trouble", you will be prepared to deal with the situation effectively.

It can be with a criminal or dealing with a "simple" traffic ticket. With what you are going to learn, you will be more alert, smart, rational, analytical, prudent, and will see everything from a different perspective of total control without being naive.

By learning the techniques of MALICE with a PURPOSE, you will be prepared at all time at home, at work or at any place you go. This method will show you the most vital points on the body of your opponent that you can hit to NEUTRALIZE them, and you will become more conscious and alert when you need to defend yourself or your loved ones.

It will give you a sense of security and self-confidence to know that you will need just ONE movement to hit only ONE of those vital points if you need to and without drawn out a long fight or looking for an instructor to teach you how to defend yourself *after* you were hurt because you did not know how to act in such situation before.

As an expert in security, self-defense and forensic sciences and by dealing with cases of all kind of criminals and very bad people, I saw that many people found out that to be effective in protecting themselves it was necessary to spend a lot of time practicing the skills and taking classes. The average person does not have the time or money to take martial arts training courses. And in some cases, it will take years to master those techniques.

In addition to this, most of the classes are for the martial arts in which you need to learn certain rules. Rules that will not be practiced by your ENEMY outside the classroom in the event of a physical confrontation, giving them the great advantage against you.

I served in the most prestigious security system of the State of Israel as the Security Coordinator and Bodyguard for diplomatic entities, where your alertness, intuition and reaction are very important to save your life or the life of the person you are protecting and being ALERT is the first one.

Here, I will teach you how to take the security measures necessary for a safer life within your home, on the streets and anywhere else you go, because being too naive is not good and the results are bad and they can imply physical harm, jail, loss of money and even death to you or your loved one.

Sometimes, some of these measures I will discuss are heard by your parents or close friends, but they will not tell you because they see malice as something bad and not as something for protection. But when things happen, they are the first ones to say, "I should have told you, but now it is too late."

Also, being too "suspicious" about everyone is not good either. It can be seen, as a paranoid personality. Being ALERT and ANALYTICAL concerning new people close to you and lifting a red flag on them until you get to know that person is a plus in making the right or the wrong decision and this includes places where we go or when we are dealing with some "professionals" or services where you can get "trapped" in a one-way contract or relation for the lack of malice and once again being naive because you didn't know.

The MALICE with a PURPOSE method, techniques and procedure; was developed while taking into consideration the high percentage of crimes. Crimes which are affecting so many people in both big and small cities and countries. Lots of evil people with malice are using their "abilities" to affect others with their bad intentions. With the information presented to you here you will feel safe and self-reliant in just minutes after following these instructions.

Malice with a Purpose will cover topics like prevention and confrontation in a short, clear and easy way to understand. Read and remember these procedures so you will have

them available in case you need to use them. Remember, it is your "stealth weapon" of self-defense. My emphasis and repetitions here are just because I want you to keep them in mind, so you will have them "there" when you most need them.

Here you will learn the most important physical weakness points of any man other than the groin. You will learn...

- ...how to recognize an aggressive behavior BEFORE it is too late.

- ...how to develop the "INTUITION" for self-defense. Because when you are with your family, you are "relaxed," but when you are in the "jungle of the streets," you will need the intuition of self-defense.

- ...how to observe the people around you, their faces, the micro-expression, body language. You will learn to make connections between suspicious looking people and their total behavior in general, which is the "base behavior" of a typical criminal.

- ...how to know when someone is lying or plans to attack you or to do you harm. You can spot the intentions of any person by looking at their body language as I will teach you here. It is like being a "walking lie detector" that can spot bad people before they act against you.

Remember that no one will tell you that they are going to attack you unless he is an idiot. You will need to analyze their body language, so you can recognize when people are going to become aggressive or planning something against you. You will learn how to identify that behavior before it hits you in the face. To do this you must be ALERT and aware of your environment at all time, maintaining an analytical mind and avoiding being NAÏVE, but being alert.

After you get used to being alert and analytical, your mind will react in an automatic form. Being alert will become just part of your personality. Remember that your mind, your body, and your heart are part of your temple as a human being. So, protect them.

You will also learn how to obtain an attitude of respect from others.

Most of the time, it is YOUR behavior that determines how other people treat you. If you are not satisfied about the treatment you are receiving, we will teach you how to change that, so you can raise your level of self-confidence and self-esteem. Remember that if you change the way you think, you will change the way you act. To do that, you will need discipline. Discipline is a matter
of doing the small but good things first, then the good big things will follow.

How to protect yourself in your home, street or car. Most of the time, people do not care enough about

their surroundings to pay attention to, because
"nothing" has ever happened to THEM before. In
their mind, they subconsciously believe that they are
"immune" until it DOES happen. Learn from the
experience of others, not from becoming the victim of
others.

Be more alert when outside of your home. One
"small" habit that I have when driving is that I think
the car behind me is always a police car. I think that
way thinking could be the main reason why I have
never had a traffic ticket. It could happen at any time,
but being alert pays a lot even with small things. The
same thing happens when you think that you can be hit
by other cars and you drive defensively or thinking that
someone can take your purse that you left in the car
while you go to pay for gasoline. Even worse, they can
take your car with your baby that you left in it. See,
these are not "small" things?

Also, carjacking happens very often when people
stop in places where criminals know that the victims
will be stopping.

I would also like to mention here that it is also very
naive for women to run in shorts in solitary places,
thinking that they are 100% confidence that nothing
can happen to them because they have the right to run

at anytime, anywhere and with the clothes they choose. This thinking could lead to tragedy.

While women should have the freedom to exercise as they choose, there are thousands of women who have been raped or kidnapped and still missing to this days. So, be careful, because what you know is your right, for criminals it is their opportunity and they don't care about your rights.

Here, you will learn how to defend yourself EFFECTIVELY and prevent dealing with toxic people that may come across you.

Remember that this is not a method of fighting techniques. This is a method of how to neutralize your attackers in less than ONE second BEFORE they attack you and how to be aware of the people you are in contact with, so you can choose the correct ones and avoid the toxic ones.

Also, how to conduct yourself when dealing with the aggressive or toxic behavior of some people. So, fell the passion of what you are going to learn here and trust yourself. By visualizing yourself at a level of respect and specially self-respect. People will notice it soon, and you will start a new life with a new level of self-confidence.

> Recognize TOXIC people and get away from them, even if they are members of your family.

---WARNING---

The contents of this book are ONLY intended for the use of responsible adults age 18 years or older. The use of this method, techniques or procedures taught here is for self-defense ONLY and intended to provide information that can be used in case of IMMINENT DANGER OF DEATH OR SERIOUS BODILY HARM against you or your loved ones, as well as to learn how to handle difficult situations with a wise mentality without being NAIVE and caught off guard by the malice of others.

Never start a fight to resolve a problem. Always abide by the law. Nevertheless, it is important to remember that you have the right to defend yourself from any unjustified physical attack, as well as to defend others in your presence.

Some of the techniques presented here can KILL, so be aware that the MALICE presented here is with the intention of self-defense only and not to do harm to others who don't do bad or illegal felonious things to you.

You will also learn several DAILY life strategies for the negative and confrontational situations that occur almost every day without any sign in advance and where you don't have the tools to handle them immediately. Be prepared, be SMART.

MALICE with a Purpose is NOT about teaching you to be MALICIOUS, but to show you the "tools" that you can use to defend yourself in case you have to. This learning will be like the "microchip" that will give you the alternatives of protection according to the situations that you may come across. Being NAÏVE cost a lot, so be SMART.

Onofre Jusino

Don't JOKE with STRANGERS. Some WORDS could be an attack to them if they are TOXIC.

STEP-BY-STEP

You will now learn in chronological order, how to escape a physical attack by AVOIDING certain people, places and situations. Then you will learn what to do when you face an imminent PHYSICAL confrontation.

First, use common sense and avoid places when your INTUITION warns you that there could be danger of a physical attack in areas or places that are unfamiliar to you or have high crime rates like dark and solitary areas, such as parks, beaches, swimming pools, solitary roads, trails, etc. Also bars without guards and a reputation for fights or drugs users and places where drug addicts hang around looking for victims to rob, to rape or to kill.

It is also wise to avoid HEATED discussions with fanatical people. Fanatics NEVER listen and NEVER understand, so an angry or HEATED discussion could lead to an aggressive, physical confrontation or trouble with the police, court, lawsuit, etc. So calm down even when you know that you are correct and when you recognize the other person as toxic. Also avoid discussions with irrational people, and believe me, there are a lot of them out there.

This reaction does not mean that you are backing up even when you are right. This means that in that moment it is not worth it because you are dealing with a toxic or irrational person. Toxic or irrational people never listen because they want to do things their way, even when they are wrong. So, move on.

You need to choose your battles as a wise person and remember that the toxic person will always find the wrong person to mess and you will have the opportunity to notice that you did it right and the toxic one found his wrong person. It is called KARMA.

The best way to avoid aggressive people is to think twice before trusting anyone. First, observe, listen and analyze. Always see them with a red flag of precaution and wait until you get to know the person well. If you just trust everyone you meet as soon as they approach, you are wasting your capacity to GET TO KNOW that person better.

If you make the wrong decision, you have allowed a TOXIC person into your life. Wait, take your time and as I mentioned before, observe, listen and analyze them before making your choice. BE SMART, and, don't waste your time and effort with the TOXIC people around you. FOCUS ON THE GOOD ONES because at the end of the day, what you need is good, quality people and not a large quantity of the bad ones. Don't do what foolish people do. Be Smart.

Specific TOXIC people that you should avoid are those with high levels of insecurity or envy. Those who want to show off at ANY expense especially yours. Some of these people are easier to spot than others. Always be observant of how people talk, move, react, laugh, ask, look, dress and how they shake your hand; (aggressive, soft, firm), etc.

Not any one of the above observations will give you the conclusion of your analysis but the combination of all of them. After having that combination, you can add or subtract the red flags that were thrown up on the new person in front of you. So, you can decide if that person should be closer or further from you. Be smart.

Be aware of people with high levels of jealousy and insecurity and those who demands your attention and or company at all time NO MATTER WHAT, because if you do not avoid these people, it will result in very big problems. They will take your time and do things that will fill you up with a lot of garbage that will intoxicate your mind sooner or later.

The best way to get rid of this kind of person is by cutting communication with them as soon as possible. I mean IMMEDIATELY, and if you can't, then go step by step. If there are a lot of phone calls from that person, set up YOUR time of talking, like 1 minute and then tell them that you have other things to do. Never say that you will call them back. Send them to the voice mail or block them. Tell them that you are reading a great book of 900 pages which is a collection of 5 other books and you just started reading it.

They will re-focus their attention on another "friend" because what they need is a listening ear. I used to tell this kind of person that they need to go to some psychologist or psychiatrist to vent all those emotions. They never called me back.

A Sociopath, is someone, who is ALWAYS in rebellion with the authorities and they refuse to follow rules and/or the law. They are mostly found in jails with lack of discipline, respect, and even have irrational behavior. For them, everything needs to be immediately, easy, and be their way. It is an impulsive behavior without controls and they don't care about almost anything. They don't follow the rules. They are very unstable, and you need to spot them before they spot you and use you. Sociopaths typically get angry at anything. They do a lot of protesting for any reason.

They don't care about discipline, the laws, rules, regulations or policies, it is just a matter to them. Be aware because there are a lot of them "looses".

A Psychopath is someone that does not experience the same feelings and emotions that you can see and perceive in normal people, they think only about themselves, and their emotions are only connected with something they hate about others. Psychopaths are typically lonely, they don't socialize with "normal" behavior, they always have something in mind that is a priority and they wait for the opportunity to act. Their acts are usually disastrous to other people's lives. They usually are not heard by their neighbors, co-workers or family. They always think about themselves.

They have their own world and usually they are very quiet and emotionless. Be careful because if something "triggers" them, it could be fatal. These are the typical serial rapist or murderers. Not all of them are in jail or in mental institutions, and of course, not all of them are males.

They are very manipulative when they want something and very aggressive if they don't get it. So, just put a red flag up to everyone until you "see" inside of that person's mind and find out their intentions. If you see that the person doesn't talk lot, don't think that it is because he is just a quiet person, a good person, or a "sweetheart." Just don't imagine anything and never the best, until you see the rest of their behavior and if you don't see it, it is time not to walk away but to run away.

Always lock the doors of your home and encourage your children to do so as well.

At night, never leave out a knife or any other sharp utensil that could be used as a weapon for an unexpected "visitor" or rapist that may surprise you in the middle of the night.

If you live alone and don't have a legal license for a weapon to protect yourself and your family, it would be wise to have long distance pepper spray accessible. You can find some that can shoot as far as 15 feet away. If the pepper hits the EYES of the intruder who comes to do harm to you and your children, he will be very disappointed, so be smart and be prepared for the unexpected.

Also, believe it or not, there are some good bow and arrows that are very inexpensive out there, especially those used to hunt. It will help if you practice as a hobby for a short period of time. But you need to always be careful with guns or the bow so as not to not shoot and hit one of your family members living in the same house. Just be careful and have a professional to teach you how to use any weapon. I once knew a woman who was a physician, and she lived alone. She kept a very long, sharp MACHETE beside her bed as her weapon for self-defense. See, it is a matter of having something close to you at home that you can reach for fast, in case of an emergency, without having to think about it at that moment what to grab to defend yourself. So be ready for an emergency before it is too late.

While in your car, ALWAYS use the safety lock and NEVER give a ride to a person you don't know or don't trust. Remember to RED FLAG everybody. Sometimes you give a ride to people who could be a friend of the wrong person. Now you will be riding with someone who is a toxic person by association. If that person has some enemies looking for him, to kill and they find him, you will go with him too, but to the morgue.

If the person has a weapon without a permit, is on probation, is a fugitive, or has drugs in his possession, and you are stopped by the police, then you will be an accomplice, and you will be charged with crimes. Your vehicle will be confiscated as well and that is being NAIVE or worse. Following that is the booking, bond, court, criminal record, the news, a lawyer, expenses, the bills, your friends, family, co-workers, the job, stress, your goals, spouse, etc.

.

When in doubt, KEEP YOUR MOUTH SHUT!
When your GUT talks to you, just LISTEN.

How to Obtain Respect from Others

To develop a respectful behavior from others towards your person, you first need to RESPECT YOURSELF. Decide to be a trustworthy person. You can do this by gaining credibility in what you SAY and DO. Fulfill your commitments and responsibilities. You will then begin to respect yourself and will feel very comfortable with the "new" you. Remember that if you change the way you think, you will change the way you act and that is called discipline. So, start doing those small but good things that are around you, including smiling at people, talking less about yourself, listening, focusing on the right people and goals, and looking for new places with excellent people to whom you can talk. You could initiate conversation with a greeting and then seek to engage them on a discussion on a relevant topic.

This behavior will provide you with a different way to see yourself and others will also begin to view you with respect. If you always behave like a clown, joking and fooling around in even SERIOUS or DANGEROUS situations, then you will see as a "puppet" or a fool by everyone around you. Behave like an adult, not as a child and you will see the difference in a very short period. Be ASSERTIVE, and if by the contrary, you find that the person you meet is a clown, a toxic one, or doesn't have the behavior you were expecting, just admit it to yourself and change directions just saying Hi to that person and move on until even the Hi to him goes away.

Begin your new personality by taking on responsibility with pride and integrity. Treat situations with the gravity that they merit. BE a person of CREDIBILITY and follow these essential tips.

BEFORE accepting someone's friendship, see how that person conducts himself. Observe their body language, the way they speak (tone of voice, aggressive or vulgar language, lack of respect, a big mouth, etc.) The way to "stop" that person from getting familiar with you or trying to strike up a friendship, is by employing

> **Always have an INTELLIGENT MENTOR on your side. Someone who can see the things that you don't see.**

what is known as the "POKER FACE." Do not allow your face to show emotions. Do not smile or show acceptance of anything that person does or says. This way you will not be giving them the opportunity to have you on their "side." DO NOT immediately respond to them or share your opinions. Remember the RED FLAG.

BE QUIET as you analyze their behavior. AFTERWARDS, you can decide if that person is TOXIC or non-toxic and whether to consider them for the opportunity to be a pre-friend. GOT THE POINT? So, choose friends, NOT enemies. Do so by observing people with an ANALYTICAL MIND and then decide if that person will become a part of your life or not. BE SMART and USE YOUR HEAD. You can also do some practice by going to different shopping malls and observe people doing things. Just observe them and their body language and you will see from a different perspective how people behave even when you are not listening to their conversation. You will start spotting a lot of behaviors that you did not notice.

Always be POLITE and COURTEOUS when you speak with others. Never display a BAD ATTITUDE. You may be doing so with the wrong person and messing with the wrong person is not what intelligent people do. So, THINK before spouting off your mouth like a machine gun shooting in all directions. If you do so, it WILL have negative consequences.

Learning to avoid all kinds of negative, verbal confrontation is the BEST way to prevent PHYSICAL confrontation. So be careful of your words and tone of your voice.

The same thing happens when you look for friends on different social websites. CHECK THEM OUT before you accept them. Take time to FILTER that person before it is too late. Investigate the kind of friends that the person has on their web page. Take note of the kinds of words they use and the things they write so you can learn about what is in their HEAD before it is too late to DELETE them. Make the best choice in the beginning of the friend-selecting process so you won't be disappointed. ALWAYS BE ALERT AND THINK SMART.

ALWAYS study the people around you in a VERTICAL way, not HORIZONTAL. This means that there are some people who can be closer to you than others, so look at them as a line in front of you. In that line, give them an imaginary number, the person with number one will be the most trusted person and the number ten or one hundred, will be the person farther from you in terms of trust.

Also, if the number one person shows you a red flag, put them with the number ten person or even farther away. Do this because all people do not behave equally. Remember that people do not hold the same ethical, psychological or moral values.

There are some people who you can have a closer relationship with and there are others that it is better to stay VERY far away. I am speaking of TOXIC people that bring PHYSICAL AND PSYCHOLOGICAL harm to others, especially to you, so keep them away from you and this may include some of your FAMILY members. Just talk as little as possible. Remember that if you want to change your life for good, you need to make changes concerning the people around you. Bad people around you are equal to trouble sooner or later.

Be SELECTIVE and don't trust ANYONE, until you get to know that person.

How to Deal with Bullies

What is a bully? How do they act and why? How can you recognize a bully intent on victimizing you or someone else?

A bully is a person who aspires to pester, trap or harass another person for a plethora of different reasons. Some of these reasons are: envy, jealousy, prejudice, fanaticism and/or competitiveness. It could be the result of some type of mental problems such as an emotional maladjustment or insecurities resulting from abusive treatment that they received as a child. Bullies are usually people who, because of the emotional maladjustment, tends to project hostility, forcefulness, arrogance and mockery towards others. These aggressive individuals are

product of their own personal insecurities. Occasionally, the bullies manifest themselves plainly and in such a way that their victim is aware of and can easily see what the bully is doing. However, it is also possible and extremely common that bullies, employs more pathological tactics. They will carry out their plans in secret, playing mind games, with whomever sees their "opponent." Another typical characteristic of bullies is that they will invest a large amount of their private time in vengeful thoughts towards the object of their harassment. Talking about bad things, even invented or exaggerated ones behind the person's back. Bullies have a pathological obsessive-compulsive disorder condition, and if you don't react on time, they will mess with your life. So, keep reading to learn what to do with bullies.

There are various maneuvers that may be used when you are attacked or pursued by a bully that differ according to the circumstances of the situation. They include communicating with the person about the discomfort he or she is causing with their continuous attacks, behavior or insults. This should be done in person or in a written form. If the person doing the harassment (the bully) is a supervisor, co-worker, contractor or client, you should IMMEDIATELY report this to the highest level of the organization where you work. Do it verbally and in writing to the President with a copy to the Human Resources Director, keep a copy with you. By doing this, you will be making a psychological and legal barrier that will bring you respect from the insane (toxic) people in the work place.

DON'T BE AFRAID, DO IT. If the problems continue, immediate legal action is recommended on behalf of the affected person or persons. First go to a psychologist to explain how stressful your life has been because of this bully, inform the psychologist that your sleeping, family, relationships, children, work, and other areas have been affected by the actions of the bully and you are suffering a lot. Those are the psychological DAMAGES caused by the bully that you will be using as EVIDENCE in court.

It is extremely necessary that when a bully maintains a threatening, obsessive and compulsive behavior with remote or no possibilities of desisting said behavior, to procure the nastiest (aggressive) lawyer that you can find. Do this, so that in the event of going to court to sue, you can make sure that your lawyer will make the bully's life miserable to such an extent that he/she never tries to bully you again and this will include the company where you work and their officers. Also, it is recommended to do a confidential and deep investigation of the past and present "life" of the bully, so you can give the information to your lawyer. Look for EVERYTHING concerning that TOXIC person. Take your time doing this, so when you have the time to act, your lawyer can "beat the shit out of them" in a wonderful manner. Bullies are big-mouthed people but really, they are afraid to fight physically. They project themselves as very tough and intimidating even when it is not necessarily the case. If you have a confrontation with this type of person, my advice is to use the techniques that you will learn about here in Malice with a Purpose.

If you don't do anything, the compulsive obsession of the bully will drive you "crazy" day and night and at the end you will have no evidence to show to the police, your lawyer or court. The behavior of the bully will mutate with a worse reaction against you, so be prepared from day one and keep a record of everything in a chronological order of what I call "idiot proof evidence" to present in court. Always think from your point of view but also try to imagine the point of view of your adversary, so you can see the possible strategies of him and you can make the necessary moves to protect yourself. It is like thinking as a Chess Player, always ahead of the opponent.

Always try to write your "report" to your lawyer so he can have a "visual" image of the case. In that report look to answer the WHAT, WHERE, WHEN, WHO, HOW AND WHY. Which are the typical questions of all kinds of investigations.

> Don't have ANIMOSITY with those who don't oppose you. Don't look for UNWANTED enemies.

How to Read a Person's Body Language and Avoid a Confrontation

If you want to learn how to read the behavior of another person, first you need to be able to read yourself. Begin by observing what you do when you speak with others. Try to observe YOUR OWN body language with people you love, people you hate, people with whom you are indifferent and people of whom you are afraid or nervous around. If you do this, you will start to learn how to read others through their body language. You can start by studying, analyzing and using your INTUITIVE PERCEPTION in these five areas:

Eyes contact

Less eyes contact means less credibility when it is part of the next areas that follows.

Time lapse in answering questions

When someone is lying, they need time to make up their mind about what they are going to say, and you can see them "filling" those spaces with movements

from their bodies that don't match up with what they
are saying.

Lack of sincerity

You will sense this lack of sincerity with a feeling or
when your intuition tells you that something doesn't
add up in general terms. Here your GUT will let you
know.

Facial and body expressions

These are involuntary movements of the eyes,
mouth, face, fingers, legs, feet, etc. When there is
"irregular tension" in the body that seems to contradict
the person's words, there will be some movement from
those parts of the body as projection of the tensions
that they produce.

Micro-expressions

These are some very small movements of body
tissues that are part of the tension produced in some
specific moments of the conversation and this happens
because there is a "fight" or contradiction of what the
person is saying and his neuro-muscular system. To
observe those micro-expressions, you will need to be
very conscious of them at the same moment that you
are asking questions. It takes some practice, but once

you learn to pay attention you will see them. So, practice by looking at some politicians when they talk on the television.

Look at those that you don't know so you don't get biased by the party that they represent. Also, you can observe the way criminals talk on television shows. The intention here is to help you to learn how to analyze people when they are lying. Look for their reactions AFTER they give the answer. In that small space AFTER the answer you will see the reaction from their bodies if they are lying.

Tone of voice

Sadness is usually expressed in a low tone of voice while happiness, love, excitement and anger are expressed in a high tone. Unless the person is working something out in his mind, they will use different tones of voice. Sometimes manipulators use a "sweet" tone of voice combined with a smile, and the difference of the manipulators versus genuine people is that you can spot by the negative micro-expression of one versus the full sincerity of the other. Just pay attention.

Take time to consider the following scenarios:

Before a physical confrontation occurs, the bad guys will always try to take advantage of the person that they are going to confront, rob, rape or harm. That advantage is found by them by first studying the area around their victim. For example, an optimal area for a crook would have a lack of police presence, lighting and people. In the case of people being present, they would be distracted and/or paying attention to something else.

Those are the main scenarios in which people are assaulted. To avoid them, you need to be ALERT by observing what is around you without being naive about the ABNORMAL behavior that you sense. If you sense something, it is a WARNING from your GUT, so listen to it, pay attention and take some action by leaving the place as soon as possible.

Being ALERT means that even in places where you may think you are safe could be dangerous. Therefore, you need to create the "INTUITION OF ALERTNESS". This can be done by ALWAYS observing your environment with an ANALYTICAL MIND and by that, I mean that NOT all people who approach you with a smile necessarily have good intentions.

Some crooks are just like a PIRATE SHIP with an idiot flag to deceive the person and make them to trust until they can attack you. So, you need to trust your gut concerning people that you don't know. It is a fact that your enemy will come as a wolf dressed in sheep's clothing and you must be alert. When things happen, your mind will go back and will tell you how naive you were, even when you felt it in your gut.

Most assaults happen when you least expect them. Maintaining an ALERT mind is like having a personal "radar" of intuition to protect you and your loved ones. So, be alert and don't trust your past "immunity" of not having a bad experience ever in your life. No one is immune to any tragedy, but those who are naive are the most affected by the "virus" of toxic people doing harm to good people. Be prepared, start to create your layers of defense.

Also, it is very important to remember that when some liars are caught lying, but they are not unrepentant, they will say that "it will not happen again." Be careful, because if you just listen and trust, but don't look at their body language, what they are saying is just an excuse to "fix" the lie to get a better manner to present it in a different way. It is just a "mutation of the lie" presented differently. Don't be NAIVE. You will see what I am telling you when you read other chapters of Malice with a Purpose and will learn by the experience of others instead of your own.

Take your time to ACT.
Acting by EMOTIONS or
ANGER will get you into trouble.

PHYSICAL CONFRONTATION

You may find yourself in the situation of an unavoidable fight. When you cannot avoid a confrontation with a person and are unable to leave the place where you are, or can't call the police or have another person to deal with the situation if possible and the ONLY alternative that you have is to confront the attacker, you will need to be CALM and EMOTIONLESS because when emotions go UP, reasoning goes DOWN. You will need to concentrate on the 3 main factors of self-defense, which are the following:

WHEN to Attack

ALWAYS ATTACK BY SURPRISE. This will give you an advantage because your assailant will think that he/she has the situation under control (since they are the one looking for the fight). By attacking FIRST, you will catch them by surprise and claim an advantage.

NEVER show any emotion before the attack. Your opponent doesn't need to know what you are going to do in advance, so SURPRISE THEM.

WHERE to Attack:

The other places beside the groin that are vital, and I recommend as very sensitives to attack are:

- The eyes
- The throat
- The solar plexus
- The lower abdomen
- The sides of the neck
- And of course, the groin

HOW to Attack

If you attack the eyes, use your fingers, a pencil, a pen, keys, etc. The eyes are one of the most sensitive areas of the body and the enemy will not have the opportunity to see you again if you do a "good job" in this part.

If you attack the throat, use ALL of your fingers held together or the side of the palm of your hand. The throat is very sensitive and a hit to that part can kill a person. Your intentions should always be to defend yourself and not to kill the enemy, BUT, if he dies it will be the result of his illegal actions against you. You were just protecting yourself.

For an attack against the solar plexus, use your fist. The solar plexus is also a very sensitive area and a hit there can throw the person to the ground because his breathing will be affected.

For the groin, use your feet, fist or knee or grab and pull them off if you are held by the attacker.

To attack the sides of the neck, use your fist or the side of the palm of your hand. In that part of the neck there is a muscle that is very sensitive to pressure or a sharp blow. If you hit hard, the attacker will fall fast.

ALWAYS HIT HARD. Remember, you are NOT going to fight, you are going to defend yourself with ONE hit only, so make it count. If you are not physically fit, I recommend that you attack the EYES of your assailant. In that case you will only need to "touch" them with your fingers, pencil, pen, etc. But do it FAST. Use your hand from the same place where you have it, don't make any movement backward with your hand like if you were to throw a punch, because that will give your enemy the opportunity to block your attack. Just move your hand from the SAME place that you it and very fast. Send two of your fingers to the eyes of your opponent and you will see how wonderful you feel after defending yourself effectively.

You MUST do this as FAST as you can, but first try to show a face of weakness and being "afraid", so your attacker will feel like in total control. Then give a small smile to "confuse" the concentration of the attacker for a moment and attack fast and hard. Always employ the element of surprise, and after the attack, move out quickly because you already have total control of the situation.

Remember that one of the elements of surprise could simply be SMILING before you attack so that your opponent feels relaxed and off guard. Then STRIKE FAST AND HARD. If you decide to use your fist to attack the face, do it by surprise and to the SIDE of the jaw. That is a very sensitive area of the face and the person will fall immediately if you hit hard enough. When defending yourself from an attacker, don't be shy during the attack. Be "generous" and do it HARD.

Don't TALK TOO MUCH
or you will show your weakness and
plans to your ENEMIES.

IF THE ENEMY HAS A WEAPON

If your enemy has a weapon, particularly a firearm, stay CALM and do not express your emotions. Remember that the target could be your possessions and not you. In this case "cooperate" with the TOXIC one until leaves or gives you the ultimate OPPORTUNITY to act. Never try to confront an armed enemy. Always use patience and self-control.

If you must talk to him or answer his questions, do it softly and keep it short. BE POLITE. He will be thinking about getting what he wants in as short a time span as possible. The principal enemy of a criminal is time because if he takes too long he could get caught. Do not OVER-cooperate with or OVER assist the enemy, because that will make them want to stay and try to take more, including you and cause more harm.

TIME IS your friend, so do not OVER talk to the enemy or do anything unless you have the COMPLETE OPPORTUNITY TO ACT. Try to be rational, not emotional, so you can act with logic.

If the person has a knife, you can use any object close to you to defend yourself, such as your belt, but in that case, use the BUCKLE to hit. It will be more effective than the leather.

Don't WASTE your time TALKING to IRRATIONAL or EMOTIONAL people about your GOALS.

What to Do if You Have a Weapon

THESE MEASURES ARE FOR THOSE WHO HAVE A LEGAL WEAPONS AND MAY NEED TO USE IT.

If you find yourself in a situation where your life or the life of any other human being is in IMMINENT DANGER OF DEATH or SERIOUS BODILY HARM, by law you are entitled to DEFEND yourself or DEFEND the human being in danger. If, to do that you need to use your legal weapon, USE IT.

If the person you are confronted by has a weapon, just be calm and FIRE FIRST. Don't open your mouth to speak because that may alert the person, allowing him to shoot you first. The Talmud states, "If a man intends to kill you, strike first."

Don't discharge the weapon against the attacker if it is not necessary and by necessary, I mean that if the person falls after being hit. Continuing to shoot at an attacker can be considered voluntary manslaughter. So, never over shoot or "over kill." That way you can show that you only had the intentions to defend yourself. But if the person keeps the weapon in his hand, then keep defending yourself with your weapon until there is no danger to your life.

NEVER use a weapon to shoot into the air or to scare someone away. NEVER shoot when there are other people around you because you do not know where your bullet will stop. Stray bullets could harm or kill an innocent bystander. Also remember that a bullet can penetrate most wooden walls or even ricochet, which means that the bullet can hit some hard surface and change direction and hit someone very far away without you noticing it.

If you fire a weapon at someone of course with good reason, ask someone close by to call 911. Tell them that they need to ask for an ambulance and the police because someone has been shot. IF YOU MAKE THE CALL, REMEMBER THAT EVERYTHING YOU SAY WILL BE RECORDED by the 911 operating system. They will also ask questions which could cause you to unintentionally give up your right to remain SILENT by talking too much. Whatever you say can be used against you in court, so it is better to have someone else make the call. Before you speak TO A POLICE OFFICER, REQUEST A LAWYER, because it is your constitutional right. (5TH Amendment of the Constitution of the United States of America)

With the police, always be COURTEOUS AND POLITE. Immediately provide them with your name, address and phone number and then tell them that YOU WANT A LAWYER BEFORE YOU CONTINUE TO SPEAK WITH THEM. IT IS YOUR LEGAL RIGHT. If the Police ask you why you need a lawyer, just tell them it is because it is your right and then, BE QUIET, SHUT UP, SILENCE.

Sometimes people talk because they want to show that they are not hiding anything and that what they did was correct. The problem is that things can get distorted especially in a police report and once that is done, you are caught with that "testimony". Any police officer can call it the "confession" that you gave at the crime scene. See, naive people do this a lot of times and then they need to find a lawyer to fight hard in court to convince the jury or the judge that you didn't say at the crime scene what the police said in his report, his statement, or in front of the jury, just because your emotions were high at that moment and you opened

your mouth. So, SHUT UP and talk ONLY to your
lawyer. Be SMART.

When in a **GROUP**,
be the last one to present
an OPINION,
so you can HEAR
the opinion of others.

WOUNDED VERSUS DEAD

When you use a firearm for your own personal defense and protection, the assailant whom you have had to defend yourself against will probably end up wounded or dead. In the case of the assailant being wounded, his or her testimony could be used as proof against you in court if the police decide to accuse you. In other words, your attacker could try to give his own version of events about the situation. This will then form part of the evidence that the police will gather together to possibly accuse you.

It is because of this, as I have stated in other cases, that you should keep quiet when being questioned by the police. Unless **you have** a trusted lawyer present, who will speak for you, but those cases are not common. In the case of the death of the person you attacked out of self-defense or to protect someone else from imminent danger of death or serious bodily harm, the police and the investigators will have to rest their investigation on multiples elements of evidences, such witness accounts, closed circuit cameras, autopsy results, toxicological reports, photos, videos, forensic analysis, ballistic analysis, DNA, fingerprints, paramedic accounts, forensic pathologist, etc. However, if this is not the case, refrain from speaking or sharing any information without the authorization of your lawyer. Again, be quiet, shut up, BE SILENT.

> When under investigation,
> be smart and SHUT your mouth.
> It is your Constitutional Right.

Interacting with the Police

When interacting with the police, remember that they will ask you questions during what will be either an interview or an interrogation. The interview and the interrogation basically have the same purpose, which is to obtain information for the police so that they can arrive at their own conclusions about what has occurred.

When they do so, they will then accuse the person they believe to be responsible for the crime and give their information to the prosecutor. An interview is usually a series of general questions about you and the crime that has occurred. These questions do not tend to be as harsh as the ones that are asked in an interrogation. In the case of an interrogation the questions about the crime
addressed will be very specific, sharp and more difficult to answer.

In both cases, my recommendation is to speak as little as possible while maintaining a courteous attitude with the police, but it is preferable to keep your mouth shut at all time. Remember that you have constitutional rights and you should use them. So, stay silent. You may say to yourself that you have the constitutional right when you are accused but not before, FALSE. You talk if you want BUT you don't have to talk and that is part of your right of Freedom of Speech, where you choose to whom you talk or not talk, and it is also a Constitutional Right that you have. Use it! Even if the police officer harasses you to talk, just be quiet.

Sometimes the police will decide to bring the person who has been detained or arrested "for investigation" to the police headquarters. Upon arrival the person will probably be brought to an interrogation room where the police officer in charge of the investigation will proceed to ask simple, general and seemingly "inoffensive" questions. They will do so in such a way that you will not perceive any kind of accusation and because of this you may be persuaded to speak. If you do so this could provide the opportunity and the space for the police to spin their case against you. Like a spider spins a web and then traps you with your own words, and <u>Everything that you say in the interrogation room will be taped in audio and video by the police investigator.</u> So, don't be so nice or naive, you are not selling something. Be Quiet. Shut up.

By ruling of the Supreme Court of the United States, the police officer or investigators are authorized to use "tricks," strategies or even deception as a part of their strategy to make you believe that they have X or Y evidence against you. So that they can induce you to confess to a felony or any other crime. Once again, my advice is to be accompanied by a LAWYER at all time and remember to KEEP YOUR MOUTH SHUT, until you have a lawyer with you. So as soon as you enter the Police Station, say "I WANT A LAWYER." Those are the most hated words of any police officer or investigator, because that will stop any questioning and/or interrogation. IMMEDIATELY.

On the contrary, when a police officer intervenes for the violation of a mere transit law, first keep your hands on the steering wheel of your car where the police officer can see them, so they don't become anxious or suspicious about you and if it is at night, turn the inside light on. Give your license, vehicle registration and insurance to the officer and avoid any argument with him, whether he is right or not.

Remember that now, by a Federal Court decision, you can video tape a police officer who interacts with you and that video and audio tape can be used as evidence if you have been mistreated or your civil rights have been violated. As soon as the officer has pulled you over and told you the infraction that he or she says you have committed, speak respectfully and with courtesy. Sincerely apologize for the matter and KEEP YOUR MOUTH SHUT! The less you talk, the best it is for you. If not, matters could become worse, magnifying the problem and escalating the situation. Don't be naive, be smart. Calm down. It could be just a ticket and not an arrest or worse.

I know of a case of a car accident in which the vehicle of one person (A), crashed into the posterior part of other car (B), resulting in a broken tail light. The damages caused could not have been more than twenty dollars.

Person (A), who provoked the accident went into an argument with the owner of the second car (person B) that was hit, because he didn't want to pay for the damages of the broken light. The driver (B) told driver (A) that if that was his position, then he would have to call the police to make a complaint.

Driver (A) said that there was no need to call the police because he was a police officer and he showed a gun that he had under his shirt. Driver (B) decided to yell to the people in the area to call the police. Driver (A) decided to use his gun to shoot driver (B) in the chest resulting in his death. This bad decision ended up costing the police officer 24 years in prison for murder, instead of twenty dollars to repair a broken light. When emotions go up, reasoning goes down.

Sometimes a bad day of stress, disappointments or just the regular bad behavior of some people can escalate and could change a simple situation that could be handled with diplomacy, politeness, courtesy, etc, to a tragic one. Words like I am sorry, I apologize, I will take care of that, don't worry, etc, can resolve a tough situation, but some NAIVE people sometimes think that words

> **Be SELECTIVE and don't trust anyone before you know them. Trust is gained with time and good acts.**

don't have meanings, and sometimes those "MEANINGS" can provoke a death sentence, like in the case I mentioned above. I interviewed this police officer and his ex-wife, and they told me that he did it because he wasn't thinking at that moment. He told me that he was full of stress and had marital problems. That acted by emotions and without control.

The above situation can happen to any person and my recommendation is to always think before you open your mouth. Make sure that when you speak, everything you say doesn't have bad repercussions and can be "heard" by your mother, children, a judge and a jury without causing you any trouble. Also, it is very important to think that a weapon doesn't give you a right above the law even if you are an officer or a civilian. I am sure that this police officer, as well as many other people rejected their behaviors when they do thing without controlling the emotions and by not thinking correctly and with prudence at the time of stress. This can happen to anyone, so practice being in control of the SMALL things and the big ones will follow.

> **Don't be NAIVE to trust
> people immediately.
> It is a MISTAKE.**

How to Choose a Lawyer to Represent You

When events occur in which persons involved could suffer legal, civil and criminal repercussions, it is very important to be assisted by a lawyer. That lawyer will need to have the sufficient knowledge, experience, expertise, interest and dedication to represent you.

It is not a good idea to hire the first attorney you come across. It is likely that if you do so, it will be because of the stress of the situation, and you just want to take your problem and pass it on to your lawyer. In the long-term, you could be throwing away your money for bad legal representation. You need to find out if the lawyer you are interested in hiring has experience in similar cases and shows interest in your case. Also, you need to ask about possible strategies and look for an attitude that demonstrates that the lawyer will represent you in an energetic and aggressive way.

It is also very important that the lawyer has the legal knowledge that the circumstances merit.

When you make a contract with a lawyer, you should make sure that an empathy exists between him/her and you. Try to get to know the "person" because they will be legally representing you in court. If the lawyer you are interviewing does not project sufficient knowledge, credibility, experience, gravity, motivation or interest, DO NOT HIRE THEM or else you will lose your case and your money.

If they give you a contract to be signed, READ IT FIRST! This includes the small writing. If you do not agree with some of the words, sentences, paragraphs or conditions in that contract, just mark through it and put your initials there as well as have the initials of the lawyer. Don't leave the office of your lawyer with any doubts. Be clear, assertive and honest, and be sure that you get the same from them.

If not, you will be taking on an additional problem. ALWAYS get a copy of the contract that you make with your lawyer. Ask if you can study it at home BEFORE you sign it. Make sure that you check the contract with an analytical mind (in detail). Also, you can consult another lawyer to get a second legal opinion.

During the first interview, as in all other interviews that you have with your attorney, pay attention to the things they say or promotes, like maintaining a clear and constant written communication with you about your case. In the eventuality that you are declared guilty and any of the agreements made with your lawyer were not kept, you can make a complaint concerning the Canons of Professional Ethics and use the MALPRECTICE of said lawyer for an appeal to a higher court. Remember that you should think twice before trusting anyone. In the case of lawyers, my recommendation is to think at least ten times, because they know the law and the WORDS that they can add or subtract from the contract that they make with you and the legal meaning of those words for their convenience.

When in their office, look how they has the documents, desk and office in general, how they handle the calls, etc. If you see that there is a mess in that office or their thoughts looks not to be clear, don't walk out, just RUN AWAY.

Also, it is very important to look for a lawyer that you feel in your gut you can trust. Don't look for "famous" or expensive lawyers. That doesn't guarantee that they will represent you professionally, ethically and legally, even when the result of your case is not the best for you, but they will do their work correctly and professionally. Sometimes the lawyer with more cases is the one who will put less time in your case because they are very busy with the rest of their OTHER cases. So be careful and think smart.

Also, in some occasions you contract the "famous" lawyer and they give your case to their NEW partner, which usually is the rookie of the office and you are paying for the knowledge and experience that you are NOT receiving. So be aware to know exactly the lawyer that will be representing you.

Before the ATTACK, always SMILE at your enemy. This will lower his defenses. Then, HIT FAST and HARD.

WITNESSES

In the eventuality of being accused of a crime, the police will most assuredly bring witnesses against you. Because of this, it is very important for you to get those witnesses investigated to find out:

- Who they are
- Their prejudices
- Their statements
- Their interest in the case
- Cases they may have had in court
- Police record of any convictions
- Lawsuits
- Educational background
- Personality

You should even investigate what they share on social media such as Facebook, Twitter, etc. All this data could be used at any point in time, to detract from the authority of these witnesses and the theory that your lawyer presents on behalf of your innocence.

Sometimes, when the case takes too long to be presented in court, witnesses forget a lot of things about the case. Such as dates, hours, people, statements and in some cases, they move to a different state, or even change their name. Their memory may be affected, and without witnesses, the case becomes weak. So, one of the typical tactics that some lawyers use in their cases is to extend their case as much as possible to look for fewer witnesses from the prosecutor's part.

Most DECISIONS can be taken with 70% of probability of SUCCESS.

WITNESSES AND EXPERT WITNESSES

In my experience from testifying as an expert witness on hundreds of occasions, I have noticed that court cases are not necessarily won by those who are right, but by those who are convincing. In other words, both, witnesses and expert witnesses do not only have to tell the truth about an event, but they need to CONVINCE the jury or the judge presiding for the case of the validity of your testimony.

Convincing or not convincing them is achieved by the methods in which the witnesses presents their testimonies. It includes the way they verbally address the court and the body language uses while speaking. If both, their verbal and body language are seen, as convincing by the judge and jury, the probability of being viewed as credible is much greater. Credibility is most important when you are testifying in court.

The experience and the knowledge displayed by the expert witness in the evaluation or the analysis made about the event which he/she has been hired to testify about, must be taken into consideration and can add or take away from the credibility of them. ALWAYS behave as a professional.

It is extremely important that the expert witness is present when you meet with your attorney. This is because he/she can learn about the case from you and the lawyer, and to have a clear comprehension of the case. So, the lawyer, the expert, your witnesses and you, should be present. When dealing with the analysis that the expert needs to do, that part belongs to his/her expertise only and only they will let your lawyer know the documents, reports, or whatever he/she needs to perform the expert analysis in which the result could be, or not, favorable to you. In other words, the Expert Witness is the one that, if needs to go to court, they will have to tell the truth under oath, and if the results of the analysis are not compatible with the theory of your lawyer, it will be better not to present them as your expert, because they will have to testify against your testimony or evidence in the opinion to the court.

The first thing that I do and recommend you do, when going to court is being on time at the court. Never late, dress properly, turn off your cellphone, be quiet, observe the judge, the jury, the prosecutor, project a calm personality Always do your movement without drawing attention to yourself, keep your keys in your pocket, don't make noises, talk only to your lawyer, don't make facial expressions. If you are called on to testify, talk loudly so everyone can hear you in the court. Never argue with anyone, even if they are wrong, just say that that is not correct. Be as natural as possible. If they ask you to answer YES or NO only and you think that the answer could be either way, just say it DEPENDS and if allowed, just explain your answer.

> **Be SELECTIVE with
> the friends you choose.
> Raise a RED FLAG until
> you get to know them.**

TESTIFYING IN COURT

In the eventuality that you testify on your own behalf in court, whether you were instructed to do so by your lawyer or decided to do so yourself, you must be prepared. Behave naturally and convincingly. Do not exaggerate. Make eye contact with the judge and the jury. Practice what you are going to say with your lawyer ahead of time. Have your lawyer play the district attorney by asking you hostile questions so that it will be less difficult when you need to answer these same questions in court. You must always be on the alert. Observe the body language of the people you are speaking to, and at the same time, be aware of your own body language, because they are observing you too.

The lawyers or the district attorney typically start their cases with questions that they can use as a base to the theory of their case. Then they spin them up to ask you the questions that are relevant for THEM. Be aware of every single question. Take your time to answer, and consider the repercussions of your answers before you speak.

Also, it is normal for lawyers to ask questions to get the same answer of YES or NO several times. They start by asking you X or Y questions, so you may answer yes 10 times or no 10 times. Then, they will come up with the question that they were "hiding," and because you already were answering in a "semi-automatic" mode, they will catch you in the last one. SEE, BE ALERT to all the questions they ask, because one of them will be the trick question and the most important one. If the lawyer yells at you or is disrespectful, mention it to the judge immediately so it is kept on record. Never get into an argument with the lawyer in front of the judge or the jury. He can be testing you or provoking you, so you react emotionally or irrational. Be careful, and remember that when emotions go up, reasoning goes down.

ALWAYS act naturally, cool, and normal. Remember you are there to win your case, and to win, you need not only to be right, but to convince. Convincing is a combination of body language, verbal language and the evidence you present.

Get the **NASTIEST LAWYER** that you can find **TO FIGHT FOR YOU** in court when it comes to fight against a **BULLY**, so he/she will **NEVER** mess with you again.

Home Security

The best way for you to protect your home is to go outside, stand in front of it and try to figure out how you would get into your house without a key and without drawing attention to yourself or anyone inside realizing that you are breaking in. In other words, do the same thing that an intruder would do if he is attempting to get into your house. You need to think about the three elements that will lead a criminal to perform a crime, and once are together, the crime will occur. Ability, Opportunity and Desire.

Pay attention to the locks, the windows, the kind of neighbors you have, alarms, and security cameras. Consider what actions to take in case someone illegally enters your home. This will help you to know what additional measures you need to take to protect your property, valuables, family, and life.

If you don't have the economic resources to have an alarm system, a dog, cameras, etc, just get some "dummy" cameras, signs of "beware of dog" and signs of an alarm system and put them around your home. These will create a dissuasive reaction from criminals. This will also help to create a psychological layer or barrier to anyone that doesn't know that they are false. If someone asks you about your new "dog," just tell them that he is very quiet, protective, and aggressive. Be smart.

Also, it is very important NOT to "rush" your invitation to your home to any person you just met without knowing that person.

I remember a case where a woman met a man, liked his personality, and after a few phone calls talking about insignificant things, she decided to invite him to visit her at her home. Luckily, her family was there, and one of her brothers got into a conversation with the "new" visitor and asked him about his life. The guy became nervous because he didn't like to talk about his life.

The brother became suspicious and kept pushing the question until he got the answer. It turn out the new "friend" was on probation for a felony case. He didn't want to mention this, and he said that it happened because at the time that it occurred, he did not have the medicines for his paranoid schizophrenic condition. The brother took this opportunity to start "cutting" the conversation and alerted his sister about the man. See, people that are on probation or have psychological illnesses need help and we shouldn't be prejudiced with them, but things can happen more often by probability than possibility and PROBABLE is closer than POSSIBLE. So, don't make the bad experiences PROBABLE by being NAÏVE.

What you are reading here, will act like a "psychological antibody," to prepare you to learn from the bad experience of others and NOT by yours.

JUDGES, LAWYERS and POLICE, are afraid of ETHICAL COMPLAINTS. Treat them with RESPECT and expect the same from them or present a WRITING COMPLAINT.

FINAL ADVICE

Always be responsible to the law and always avoid confrontation when possible. Remember that in any fight you will ONLY know what to do if you stay ALERT and ATTACK QUICKLY AND BY SURPRISE IN ONE OF THE AREAS MENTIONED in this book. By being ALERT, I mean that you need to study and OBSERVE things differently than the way you usually look at them. So be AWARE.

You need to OBSERVE people and their MOVEMENTS like a HAWK does when he looks for his prey. That is exactly the way someone may be looking at you. Don't be the prey. Remember that people "talk" with their eyes, so analyze those looks to see if they have the intention to do you harm. Trust your gut, believe me, TRUST YOUR GUT.

Practice being ALERT and it will become part of you and will help you to develop the INTUITION that makes you more aware of the danger factors of any situation or confrontation. In Israel, I found that the Jewish people are security conscious, so they can protect themselves effectively. INTUITION is their main weapon of self-defense and especially, when they are dealing with terrorists. BE ALERT and use your INTUITION.

Don't be NAÏVE; be SMART. Any place could be the wrong one, so don't give the bad guys the chance to combine their desires and ability with an OPPORTUNITY. ALWAYS BE ALERT AND TRUST YOUR GUT.

Use these advices, methods and/or techniques as your alternative to self-defense. By thinking that MALICE with a PURPOSE has the intention to protect you from the bad people that use malice ON purpose against you. Be smart and be responsible with yourself, your family and your community and NEVER BE AFRAID to defend yourself.

Read this book several times so that you can remember the important principles of self-defense and make these practices a part of your lifestyle. Review the ways that bad people abuse the good ones with scam, lack of integrity and malice. Being unaware, naive or not alert, could surprise you in different scenarios, places or moments especially when you least expect it.

This book will make you think different and will serve as a tiny "microchip" in your head that will help you to be ALERT and SMART if you are ever find yourself in a threatening situation. This knowledge is necessary for WISE and good people if they want to be safe and not regret a bad experience for them or their loved ones.

> Most people sign **CONTRACTS**
> without **READING THEM.**
> **Be SMART,** read it **FIRST.**

Some TOXIC PEOPLE to Avoid

- CRITICS WITHOUT CREDENTIALS
- ARROGANT
- PARASITES
- DIRTY MOUTHED
- DRUG ADDICTS
- ENVIOUS
- ABUSERS
- UNTRUSTWORTHY
- LAZY
- JEALOUS
- FRIENDS OF TOXIC PEOPLE
- FANATICS
- EGOCENTRIC
- MANIPULATORS
- INEPTUS
- DRUNKARDS
- CHEATERS
- INCONSIDERATE PEOPLE
- UNHYGIENICS
- TWO FACES
- AGGRESSIVES

- NARCISSISTIC
- PARANOIDS
- PSYCHOPATHS
- STALKERS
- SOCIOPATHS
- MEDDLER
- PESSIMISTICS
- UNKEMPT
- POSSESSIVE
- COMPULSIVE LIARS
- RUDE
- YES MAN
- A JERK ON STEROIDS
- OVER DRAMATICS
- BROWN NOSE
- ROWDY
- WHINER
- MOOCHER
- DISGRUNTLED

A LAWYER could be
your **ANGEL** or your
NIGHTMARE, so be **ALERT.**

NON-TOXIC, BUT BE CAREFUL

- PROSECUTORS. Their objective is to send you to jail.
- INFORMANTS. Sometimes they exaggerate things
- OVERLY QUIET PERSON. Never know what they are up to.
- OVER ANALYTICAL. They look for the minimal details.
- INVESTIGATORS. They write down everything you say.
- POLICE OFFICERS. Caution when talking. Lying to them is a crime.
- FEDERAL AGENTS. Beware of what you say to them. Lying to them is a crime.
- REPAIRMAN. Ask for credentials.
- STRANGERS. Get to know them first.
- PEOPLE TALKING OVER THE PHONE behind you.
- TEXT MESSAGES. Beware of what you write.
- EMAILS. Be careful of what you write.
- BABYSITTERS. Know them well and talk to their references.

- LAWYERS. They know the laws and the words to use.
- NEIGHBORS. Be selective when talking to them.
- PERSONAL INFORMATION in your trash can be taken.
- SALESMEN. They get a lot of information about you.
- REPORTERS. Some could be informants.

> **Always THINK about the CONSEQUENCES before they happen.**

BIOGRAPHY

Onofre Jusino is a citizen of the United States of America and the State of Israel, has a PhD in Criminology with a concentration in Criminal Psychology. He is a U.S. Army Veteran, graduated from the FBI National Academy, former: Intelligence Services Officer, Security Coordinator and Officer for the State of Israel. Director of the Israel Institute of Investigations. Police Academy Professor and Police Inspector. Judo Champion who learned and practiced different methods of self-defense for many years. He has also been a Court Qualified Forensic Expert in multiples areas of the Forensic Sciences in State, Federal and Supreme courts in more than 400 Civil and Criminal cases. He is a former University Professor at the Master's Program in Criminal Justice and author of 3 other books. Speak English, Spanish, Hebrew and some Portuguese.

Made in the USA
Columbia, SC
18 February 2018